Ancient And Modern Physics

by

Thomas E. Willson

Ancient And Modern Physics
by Thomas E. Willson

ISBN: 978-93-59956-62-6

Published by

DOUBLE 9 BOOKS
2/13-B, Ansari Road
Daryaganj, New Delhi – 110002
info@double9books.com
www.double9books.com
Tel. 011-40042856

ABOUT THE AUTHOR

Thomas E. Willson become a visionary inventor and industrialist whose pioneering contributions left an indelible mark on the fields of chemistry and metallurgy. Born in Canada inside the 1860s, Willson displayed an insatiable interest and a relentless force for innovation from a younger age. He is most renowned for his groundbreaking paintings in growing the electrical furnace, a modern generation that transformed the production of calcium carbide, an crucial issue in the manufacture of acetylene gas. Willson's ingenuity and backbone no longer best revolutionized industrial tactics however also played a pivotal function within the development of modern-day lighting fixtures, as acetylene gasoline was used for early gas lamps. His innovations had a long way-achieving implications, impacting industries inclusive of steelmaking, welding, and chemical manufacturing. Willson's legacy extends beyond his innovations; he was a trailblazer within the realm of implemented science, embodying the spirit of exploration and innovation that characterizes the extraordinary inventors of history. Throughout his existence, Thomas E. Willson exemplified the transformative power of scientific curiosity and the boundless ability of human ingenuity. His work maintains to persuade and inspire generations of scientists, engineers, and inventors, making him a incredible figure within the annals of technological development.

CONTENTS

PREFACE

The Editor of the Theosophical Forum in April, 1901, noted the death of Mr. Thomas E. Willson in the previous month in an article which we reproduce for the reason that we believe many readers who have been following the chapters of "Ancient and Modern Physics" during the last year will like to know something of the author. In these paragraphs is said all that need be said of one of our most devoted and understanding Theosophists.

In March, 1901, The Theosophical Forum lost one of its most willing and unfailing contributors. Mr. T.E. Willson died suddenly, and the news of his death reached me when I actually was in the act of preparing the concluding chapter of his "Ancient and Modern Physics" for the April number.

Like the swan, who sings his one song, when feeling that death is near, Mr. Willson gave his brother co-workers in the Theosophical field all that was best, ripest and most suggestive in his thought in the series of articles the last of which is to come out in the same number with this.

The last time I had a long talk with T.E. Willson, he said"

"For twenty years and more I was without a hearing, yet my interest and my faith in what I had to say never flagged, the eagerness of my love for my subject never diminished."

This needs no comment. The quiet and sustained resistance to indifference and lack of appreciation, is truly the steady ballast which has prevented our Theosophical ship from aimless and fatal wanderings, though of inclement weather and adverse winds we had plenty.

For many long years Mr. Willson was the librarian of the New York "World." In the afternoons he was too busy to see outsiders, but, beginning with five o'clock in the afternoon until he went home somewhere in the neighbourhood of midnight, he always was glad to see his friends. He had a tiny little room of his own, very near the top of the tremendous building, his one window looking far above the roofs of the tallest houses in the district. There he sat at his desk, generally in his shirt sleeves, if the weather was at all warm, always busy with some matter already printed, or going to be, a quiet, yet impressive and dignified figure.

The elevated isolation, both figuratively and literally speaking, in which T.E. Willson lived and worked, in the midst of the most crowded thoroughfares of New York, always made me think of Professor Teufelsdrockh on the attic floor of "the highest house in the Wahngasse." The two had more than one point of resemblance. They shared the loftiness of their point of view, their sympathetic understanding of other folks, their loneliness, and, above all, their patient, even humorous resignation to the fact of this loneliness.

Yet in his appearance Mr. Willson was not like the great Weissnichtwo philosopher. In fact, in the cast of his features and in his ways, Mr. Willson never looked to me like a white man. In British India I have known Brahmans of the better type exactly with the same sallow complexion, same quick and observant brown eye, same portly figure and same wide-awakeness and agility of manner.

Last summer I heard, on good authority, that Mr. Willson had thought himself into a most suggestive way of dealing with the problems of matter and spirit, a way which, besides being suggestive, bore a great resemblance to some theories of the same nature, current in ancient India. Consequently Mr. Willson was offered, for the first time in his life, a chance of expressing his views on matter and spirit in as many articles and in as extensive a shape as he chose. The way he received this tardy recognition of the fact that he had something to say was highly instructive. He did not put on airs of unrecognized greatness, though, I own, the occasion was propitious; he did not say, "I told you so;" he simply and frankly was glad, in, the most childlike way.

And now that I have used the word, it occurs to me that "childlike" is an adjective the best applied to this man, in spite of his portliness, and his three score and more winters.

Many a pleasant hour I have spent in the small bookroom of the great "World" building. With Mr. Willson talk never flagged. We discussed the past and the future of our planetary chain, we built plans for the true and wholesome relation of sexes, we tried to find out—and needless to say never did—the exact limit where matter stopped being matter and became spirit; we also read the latest comic poems and also, from time to time, we took a header into the stormy sea of American literature in order to find out what various wise heads had to say, consciously or unconsciously, in favour of our beloved Theosophical views. And all this, being interrupted every three minutes or so by some weary apparition from some workroom in the "World" with some such question: "Mr. Willson, how am I to find out the present whereabouts of this or that Russian man-of-war? Mr. Willson, what is the melting point of iron? Mr. Willson, when was `H.M.S. Pinafore' produced for the first time?" etc., etc. And every time, Mr. Willson got up in the leisurely manner peculiar to him, reached for some book from the shelves that lined the room, gave the desired information, and as leisurely returned to the "pranic atom," or to "come and talk man talk, Willy," or to whatever our subject chanced to be at the time.

Mr. Willson's gratitude to the Theosophical Forum for its recognition was disproportionately great. As he wrote to the Editor: "give me any kind of work, writing for you, reviewing, manuscript or proof reading, I shall do anything, I shall undertake any job, even to taking editorial scoldings in all good nature, only give me work." His devotion to Theosophical thought and work in all their ramifications was just as great, as was his freedom from vanity, his perfectly natural and unaffected modesty.

At the news of his death many a heart was sincerely sad, but none so sad as the heart of the editor of the Theosophical Forum. For a friend and co-worker like T.E. Willson, ever ready to give material help and moral encouragement, is not easily replaced.

For a soul so pure of any kind of selfishness the transition from the turmoil of life to the bright dreams of death must have been both easy and enviable. ————————

Chapter One

The Physical Basis if Metaphysics

The Hindu system of physics, on which the metaphysical thought of the East is based, does not in its beginnings differ widely from the latest physics of the West; but it goes so much farther that our physics is soon lost sight of and forgotten. The Hindu conception of the material universe, taken from the Upanishads and some open teaching, will serve for an illustration. They divide physical matter into four kinds—prakriti, ether, prana, and manasa—which they call "planes." These differ only in the rate of vibration, each plane vibrating through one great octave, with gulfs of "lost" octaves between. The highest rate of vibration of prakriti is measured by the thousand, the lowest of the ether by trillions, and the lowest of prana by—never mind; they have, and we have not, the nomenclature.

The earth, they teach, is a globe of prakriti, floating in an ocean of ether, which, as it has the sun for its center of gravity, must necessarily be a globe. This etheric sun-globe has a diameter of over 300,000,000,000 miles. All the planets revolve around the sun far within its atmosphere. The etheric sun-globe revolves on its axis once in about 21,000 years, and this revolution causes the precession of the equinoxes. This etheric sun-globe is revolving around Alcyone with other etheric globes having suns for their centers and solar systems of prakritic globes within them in a great year of 5,640,000,000 of our common years. Its orbit has a diameter of 93,000,000,000,000,000 miles.

Beyond the etheric globes, and between them, is a third form of matter called prana, as much rarer and finer than the ether as the ether is rarer and finer than prakriti. As this prana has Alcyone for a center of gravity, it is necessarily a globe; and there are many of these pranic globes floating in a vast ocean of manasa—a form of matter as much finer than prana as prana is finer than ether, or ether than prakriti. With this manasa (which is a globe) the material, or physical, universe ends; but there are spiritual globes beyond. The material universe is created from manasa, downward, but it does not respond to or chord with the vibration of the globes above, except in a special instance and in a special way, which does not touch this inquiry.

The physical universe of the ancient (and modern) Hindu physicist was made up of these four kinds or planes of matter, distributed in space as "globes within globes."

Professor Lodge in 1884 put forth the theory that prakriti (physical matter) as we call it, was in its atoms but "whirls" of ether. Since then speculative science has generally accepted the idea that the physical atom is made up of many cubic feet of ether in chemical union, as many quarts of oxygen and hydrogen unite chemically to make a drop of water. This is an old story to the Hindu sage. He tells his pupils that the great globe of manasa once filled all space, and there was nothing else. Precisely as on this earth we have our elementary substances that change from liquids into solids and gases, so on this manasic globe there were elementary substances that took the form of liquids, solids and gases. Its manasic matter was differentiated and vibrated through one octave, as the prakritic matter does on the earth. Its substances combined as that does.

One combination produced prana. The prana collected, and formed globes. On these pranic globes the process was repeated, with ether as the result, and the etheric globes formed. Then the process was repeated on the etheric globes, as the modern scientists have discovered, and prakriti and prakritic globes came into being.

The true diameter of the earth, the ancient Hindu books say, is about 50,000 miles. That is to say, the true surface of the earth is the line of twenty-four-hour axial rotation; the line where gravity and apergy exactly balance; where a moon would have to be placed to revolve once in 86,400 seconds. Within that is prakriti; without is ether. It is also the line of no friction, which does exist between matter of different planes. There is friction between prakriti, between ether, between prana; but not between ether and prana, or ether and prakriti. Friction is a phenomenon confined to the matter of each plane separately. We live at the bottom of this gaseous ocean—on its floor—21,000 miles from the surface and only 4,000 miles from the center. Here, in a narrow "skin" limited to a few miles above and below us, is the realm of phenomena, where solid turns into liquid and liquid into gas, or vice versa. The lesson impressed upon the pupil's mind by Hindu physics is that he lives far within the earth, not on it.

There is a comparatively narrow "skin" of and for phenomena within the etheric sun-globe, say the Eastern teachers, where the etheric solids, liquids, and gases meet and mingle and interchange. Within this "skin" are all the planets—the "gaseous" atmosphere of the etheric globe stretching millions of miles beyond the outermost planetary orbit. The earth is in this skin or belt of etheric phenomena, and its ether is in touch with the ether "in manifestation" on the etheric globe. The sun and other etheric globes are within the corresponding "skin" of phenomena of the pranic globes. The prana, manifesting as solid, liquid, and gas, or in combination and in forms, is in perfect touch with that of the etheric globe, and through that with the prana of the earth. That our prana is in touch with that on the pranic globe in all its manifestations means much in metaphysics. The same is true of the manasic globe, and of our manasa.

The great lesson the Eastern physics burns into the pupil is that we are living not only within the prakritic earth, but within each of the other globes as well in identically the same way and subject to the same laws. Our lives are not passed on one globe, but in four globes. It is as if one said he lived in Buffalo, Erie county, New York, United States; that he was a citizen of each and subject to the laws of each.

This question of the four globes, of the four planes of matter, of the four skins, and of the four conditions or states of all matter and necessarily of all persons, from the purely material standpoint, is not only the foundation of Oriental physics, but the very essence of Oriental metaphysics—its starting-point and corner-stone. To one who carries with him, consciously or unconsciously, the concrete knowledge of the physics, the abstract teaching of the metaphysics presents no difficulty; it is as clear as crystal. But without the physical teaching the metaphysical is not translatable.

Our Western physics teaches that physical matter is divided into two kinds prakriti (commonly called "physical matter") and ether; that the differences of each of the elementary prakritic substances (iron, copper, sulphur, oxygen) are in their molecules, the fundamental atom being the same; that each of these elementary substances vibrates only through one octave, though on different keys; that it changes from solid to liquid and gas as the rate of vibration is increased and from gas to liquid and solid as its vibration is decreased within its octave; that the ether obeys identical laws; that it has elementary substances vibrating through one octave only, and that these are solids, liquids, or gases on the etheric plane as prakriti is on this; that these etheric substances change and combine in every way that prakriti does; and that while all our prakritic substances vibrate within (say) fifty simply octaves, the lowest vibration of etheric matter begins over one thousand octaves beyond our highest, making a gulf to leap. The Eastern physics presents this with a wealth of detail that dazes the Western student, and then adds: "But beyond the etheric plane (or octave) of vibration for matter there is a third plane (or octave) of vibration called prana and beyond that a fourth called manasa. What is true of one plane is true of the other three. One law governs the four. As above so below. There is no real gulf; there is perfect continuity."

The Western scientist teaches as the foundation of modern physics that "each and every atom of prakritic matter is the center of an etheric molecule of many atoms;" that "no two prakritic atoms touch," although their etheric envelopes or atmospheres do touch; and that "all physical phenomena are caused by the chording vibration of the prakritic atom and its envelope of ether," each "sounding the same note hundreds of octaves apart." The "solid earth" with its atmosphere represents the atom with its ether. As all the oxygen and hydrogen do not combine to make the drop of water, some remaining in mechanical union to give it an atmosphere, and about one-fourth of its bulk being gas, so the atom formed of the ether does not use all the ether in its chemical union, retaining some in mechanical union for its envelope or atmosphere.

The Hindu physics goes much farther along this road. It says that, when the pranic globes were formed, each atom of prana had its manasic envelope—was the center of a manasic molecule. When the etheric globes formed, each atom of ether was the center of a pranic molecule, each atom of which was surrounded with manasa. When the prakriti was formed from the ether, each and every atom of prakriti had the triple etheric-pranic-manasic envelope. "Each and every prakritic atom is the center of an etheric molecule," says our Western science; but that of the East adds this: "And each atom of that etheric molecule is the center of a pranic molecule, and each atom of prana in that pranic molecule is the center of a manasic molecule." The four great globes of matter in the material universe are represented and reproduced in each and every atom of prakriti, which is in touch with each one of the four globes and a part of it. The same is true of any aggregation of prakriti—of the earth itself and of all things in it, including man. As there are four atoms in each one, so there are four earths, four globes, consubstantial, one for each of the four elements, and in touch with it. One is formed of prakritic atoms—the globe we know; another, of the ether forming their envelopes; another, of the prana envelopes of ether, and a fourth of the manasa around the pranic atom. They are not "skins"; they are consubstantial. And what is true of atoms or globes is true of animals. Each has four "material" bodies, with each body on the corresponding globe —whether of the earth or of the Universe. This is the physical basis of the famous "chain of seven globes" that is such a stumbling-block in Hindu metaphysics. The spirit passes through four to get in and three to get out—seven in all. The Hindu understands without explanation. He understands his physics.

The Hindu physics teaches, with ours, that "the ether is the source of all energy," but, it adds, "as prana is the source of all life, and manasa of all mind."

"When the prakritic atom is vibrating in chord with its etheric envelope," say our textbooks, "we have physical phenomena —light, heat, electricity." "Yes," says the Hindu teacher; "but when the atom and its ether and its prana are vibrating in chord, we have life and vital phenomena added to the energy. When the atom and its ether, prana, and manasa are vibrating in chord, we have mind and mental phenomena added to the life and energy." Each atom has energy, life, and mind in posse. In the living leaf the prakriti, ether, and prana are sounding the threefold silver chord of life. In the animal, the manasa is sounding the same note with them, making the fourfold golden chord of mind. Even in the plant there may be a faint manasic overtone, for the potentiality of life and mind is in everything. This unity of the physical universe with the physical atom, and with all things created—earth, animal, or crystal—is the physical backbone of Oriental metaphysics. Prakriti, ether, prana, and manasa are in our vernacular the Earth, Air, Fire, and Water of the old philosophers—the "Four Elements."

The Oriental physics has been guarded most jealously. For many thousands of years it has been the real occult and esoteric teaching, while the Oriental metaphysics has been open and exoteric. It could not be understood without the key, and the key was in the physics known only to "the tried and approved disciple." A little has leaked out—enough to whet the appetite of the true student and make him ask for more.

Chapter Two

The Two Kinds of Perception

To the savage, matter appears in two forms—solid and liquid. As he advances a step he learns it has three forms—solid, liquid and gas. He cannot see the gas, but he knows it is there.

A little further on he learns that matter as he knows it is only a minute portion of the great universe of matter—the few chords that can be struck on the five strings of his senses, and limited to one octave or key.

Whether the particular matter he investigates has a solid, a liquid, or a gaseous form depends upon its rate of vibration. If it is a liquid, by raising its rate of vibration one third it becomes a gas; by reducing it one third it becomes a solid.

Each kind of matter has vibration only through one octave. It is known to us only by its vibration in that octave. Each kind of matter has a different octave—is set on a higher or lower key, so to speak, but all octaves of vibration are between the highest of hydrogen gas and the lowest of carbon.

In mechanical compounds, such as air or brass, the rate of vibration of the compound is the least common multiple of the two or more rates. In chemical compounds, such as water or alcohol, the rate is that of the highest, the others uniting in harmonic fractions.

All matter as we know it through our senses—prakriti, as it is called in the Secret Doctrine to distinguish it from non-sensual matter—is the vibration of an universal Something, we do not know what, through these different octaves. The elementary substances (so-called) are one and the same thing—this Something—in different keys and chords of vibration; keys that run into one another, producing all sorts of beautiful harmonies.

Taking any one of these elements, or any of their compounds, all we know of it is limited strictly to its changes during vibration through one octave. What happens when the vibration goes above or below the octave has not yet been treated hypothetically.

While some elements are vibrating on higher and some on lower keys, we can consider them all as vibrating within one great octave, that octave of the universal Something which produces sensual matter, or prakriti.

But matter is not confined, we know, to this great octave, although our sensual knowledge of it is strictly confined to it. How do we know it?

Knowledge comes to us in two ways, and there are two kinds of knowledge.

1. That which comes through our senses, by observation and experience. This includes reasoning from relation.

2. That which comes through intuition—or, as some writers inaccurately say, "through the formal laws of thought."

All the observation and experience of the rising and the setting of the sun for a thousand centuries could only have confirmed the first natural belief that it revolved daily around the earth; nor by joining this experience with other experiences could any deduction have come from our reason that would have opposed it. Not our reason but our intuition said that the sun stood still and the earth revolved daily. The oldest books in existence tell us that this axial revolution of the earth was not only known in the very dawn of time but that it has been known to every race (except our own of European savages) from before the time thought was first transmitted by writing.

Ask the ablest living geographer or physicist to prove to you that the earth revolves daily and he will reply that it would be the job of his life. It can be done at great expense and great labor, but that is because we know the answer and can invent a way of showing it, not because there are any observations from which a deduction would naturally follow.

Nearly if not all our great discoveries have come to us through intuition and not from observation and experience. When we know the lines on which to work, when intuition has given us the KEY, then the observation and experience men prize so highly, and the reason they worship so devoutly, will fill in the details. The knowledge that flows from observation and the reasoning from the facts it records, is never more than relatively true, it is always limited by the facts, and any addition to the facts requires the whole thing to be restated. We never know all the facts; seldom even the more important; and reason grasps only details.

Lamarck's theory of evolution, known to all Asiatic races from time immemorial, was the intuitional and absolute knowledge that comes to all men when they reach a certain stage of development. Reason could never have furnished it from the facts, as Cuvier proved in the great debate in the French Academy in 1842, when he knocked Lamarck out, for the time being, because "it did not conform to the facts, and did not follow from any relation of the facts."

Darwin's theory of the survival of the fittest in the struggle for existence, as an explanation of the origin of species, was from observation and experience. It was based on observed facts. But Darwin was an evolutionist—a disciple of Lamarck. He held the Key. He used the Key. The value of Darwin's work does not lie in his discovering that some bugs have been derived from other bugs and that the intermediate bugs have died off. Its overwhelming value to mankind was in showing that work on the theory of evolution was correct work and that the theory was true. When the intuition of man points out the way the reason of man can follow the path and macadam the road. It usually does and claims all the credit for itself as the original discoverer.

This knowledge through intuition is absolute and exact. It is not relatively true. It is absolutely and invariably true. No additional facts will ever modify it, or require a restatement.

When Sir William Hamilton based his Logic on the dictum that "All knowledge is relative, and only relatively true," the proposition was self-evidently false. It was in itself a statement of absolute knowledge about a certain thing. It was in itself knowledge that was not relative. All knowledge could not be relative if this knowledge was not. This knowledge could not be either absolute or relative without upsetting his whole proposition, for, if relative, then it was not always true; and if absolute, then it was never true.

Sir William did not know the distinction between the two kinds of knowledge, and what he meant to say was that "All knowledge obtained by observation and experience is relative, and only relatively true."

His knowledge of this relativity was not obtained by observation or from reason. It could not possibly have been obtained in that way. It came from intuition, and it was absolute and exact. A man may have absolute and exact knowledge and yet not be able to put it into words that exactly express it to another. Hamilton had this knowledge. But it was not clearly formulated even in his own mind. He had two separate and distinct meanings for the word "knowledge," without being conscious of it.

We have yet to coin a proper word to express what comes to us through intuition. The old English word "wisdom" originally did. The old verb "wis" was meant what a man knew without being told it, as "ken" meant knowledge by experience. Try and prove by reason that a straight line is the shortest distance between two points, or that a part can never be greater than the whole, and your reason has an impossible task. "You must take them for axioms," it says. You must take them because you wis them, not because you know (ken) them.

Intuitional knowledge must not be confounded with the relative knowledge that flows through the reason: that "If the sum of two numbers is one and their difference is five," the numbers are minus two and plus three.

The point cannot be too strongly enforced that there is a distinction between the sources of what we know, and that while all we know through our sensations is only relatively true, that which we know from intuition is invariably and absolutely true. This is seen through a glass darkly, in theology, where intuition is called inspiration and not differentiated from reason.

The false notion that we can only learn by observation and experience, that the concept can never transcend the observation, that we can only know what we can prove to our senses, has wrought incalculable injury to progress in philosophy.

Because our sensual knowledge of matter begins and ends with vibration in one octave it does not follow that this ends our knowledge of it. We may have intuitional knowledge, and this intuitional knowledge is as susceptible to reason as if we had obtained it by observation.

The knowledge that comes through intuition tells us of matter vibrating in another great octave just beyond our own, which Science has chosen to name the etheric octave, or plane. The instant our intuition reveals the cause of phenomena our reason drops in and tells us it is the chording vibration of the matter of the two planes—the physical and etheric—that produces all physical phenomena. It goes further and explains its variations.

This knowledge of another octave or plane of matter comes from the logical relations of matter and its physical phenomena; but there was nothing in the observation or experience of mankind that would have led us to infer from reason an etheric plane of matter. It was "revealed" truth. But the flash of revelation having once made the path apparent, the light of reason carries us through all the winding ways. Our knowledge of the ether is not guess-work or fancy, any more than our geometry is, because it is based on axioms our reason cannot prove. In both cases the basic axioms are obtained from intuition; the structural work from reason. Our knowledge of the ether may be as absolute and exact as our knowledge of prakriti, working on physical as we work on geometrical axioms.

The recognition of the two sources of knowledge, the work of the spirit within us and of the mind within us, is absolutely necessary to correctly comprehend the true significance of the results of modern science and to accept the ancient.

Chapter Three

Matter and Ether

It is not worthwhile translating Homer into English unless the readers of the translation understand English.

It is not worthwhile attempting to translate the occult Eastern physics into the language of our Western and modern physics, unless those who are to read the translation understand generally and broadly what our own modern physics teach. It is not necessary that they should know all branches of our modern physics in all their minute ramifications; but it is necessary that they should understand clearly the fundamental principles upon which our scientific and technical knowledge of today rests.

These fundamental principles have been discovered and applied in the past fifty years—in the memory of the living. They have revolutionized science in all its departments. Our textbooks on Chemistry, Light, Heat, Electricity and Sound have had to be entirely re-written; and in many other departments, notably in medicine and psychology, they have yet to be re-written. Our textbooks are in a transition state, each new one going a step farther, to make the change gradual from the old forms of belief to the new, so that even Tyndall's textbook on "Sound" is now so antedated, or antiquated, that it might have been written in darkest Africa before the pyramids were built, instead of twenty years ago.

All this change has flowed from the discovery of Faraday that there are two states or conditions of matter. In one it is revealed by one of our five senses, visible, tangible, smellable, tastable, or ponderable matter. This is matter as we know it. It may be a lump of metal or a flask of gas.

The second condition or state of matter is not revealed by either of our five senses, but by the sixth sense, or intuition of man. This is the ether—supposed to be "matter in a very rarefied form, which permeates all space." So rare and fine is this matter that it interpenetrates carbon or steel as water interpenetrates a sponge, or ink a blotting pad. In fact, each atom of "physical" matter—by which is meant matter in the first condition—floats in an atmosphere of ether as the solid earth floats in its atmosphere of air.

"No two physical atoms touch," said Faraday. "Each physical atom is the centre of an etheric molecule, and as far apart from every other atom as the stars in heaven from one another." This is true of every form of physical matter, whether it is a lump of metal, a cup of liquid, or a flask of gas; whether it is a bronze statue or a living man; a leaf, a cloud, or the earth itself. Each and every physical atom is the centre of an etheric molecule made up of many atoms of the ether.

This duality of matter was a wonderful discovery, revolutionizing every department of science. It placed man in actual touch with the whole visible universe. The ether in a man's eye (and in his whole body) reaches in one unbroken line—like a telegraph wire —from him to the sun, or the outermost planet. He is not separate and apart from "space," but a part of it. Each physical atom of his physical body is the centre of an etheric molecule, and he has two bodies, as St. Paul said, a visible physical and an invisible etheric body; the latter in actual touch with the whole universe.

Faraday went one step further. He demonstrated that all physical phenomena come from the chording vibration of the physical atom with the surrounding etheric atoms, and that the latter exercise the impelling force on the former. Step into the sunshine. The line of ether from the sun is vibrating faster than the ether in the body, but the higher impels the lower, the greater controls the lesser, and soon both ethers are in unison. The physical atoms must coincide in vibration with their etheric envelopes, and the "note" is "heat." Step into the shade, where the ocean of ether is vibrating more slowly, and the ether of the body reduces its vibration. "The ether is the origin of all force and of all phenomena."

This etheric matter follows identical laws with prakritic matter, or, accurately, the laws of our matter flow from the etheric matter from which it is made. The ether has two hundred or more elementary substances, each atom of our eighty or ninety "elements" being the chemical union of great masses of two or more of the etheric elements or their combinations. These etheric elementary substances combine and unite; our elementary substances simply following in their combinations the law which they inherit from their parents. They take form and shape. They vibrate through one octave, and take solid liquid or gaseous form in ether, as their types here in our world take it in prakriti, as their vibrations are increased or diminished. In short, the ether is the prototype of our physical or prakritic world, out of which it is made and a product of which it is.

As this ether is "physical" matter, the same as prakriti, one harmonic law covering both, and as this ether fills all space, Modern Science divides physical matter into two kinds, which, for convenience in differentiation, are here called prakritic and etheric.

Matter is something—science does not know or care to know what—in vibration. A very low octave of vibration produces prakriti; a very high octave of vibration produces ether. The vibration of prakriti ends in thousands; that of ether begins in billions. Between them there is a gulf of vibrations that has not yet been bridged. For that reason science divides matter into two "planes," or octaves, of vibration—the matter of this visible and tangible plane being called prakriti and that of the invisible and intangible plane being called etheric. Across this gulf the two planes respond to each other, note for note, the note in trillions chording when the note in thousands is struck. Note for note, chord for chord, they answer one another, and the minutest and the most complex phenomena are alike the result of this harmonic vibration, that of the ether supplying Force and that of the prakriti a Medium in which it can manifest.

This knowledge of ether is not guesswork or fancy, and, while it is as impossible of proof as the axioms of geometry, it is worthy the same credence and honor. We are working on physical axioms exactly as we work on geometrical axioms.

Modern science represents each and every prakritic atom as a globe like the earth, floating in space and surrounded by an atmosphere of ether. "The subdivision of prakritic matter until we reach etheric atoms chemically united to make the physical unit" is the correct definition of an atom. The prakritic physical atom has length, breadth and thickness. And it has an atmosphere of ether which not only interpenetrates the atom as oxygen and hydrogen interpenetrate the drop of water, but furnishes it with an envelope as the oxygen and hydrogen furnish the drop of water with one.

Each physical atom is the centre of an etheric molecule composed of many etheric atoms vibrating at a greater or lesser speed and interpenetrating the atom. Each may be considered a miniature earth, with its aerial envelope, the air, penetrating all parts of it.

The etheric plane of matter not only unites with this prakritic plane through the atom but it interpenetrates all combinations of it; beside the atom as well as through the atom. The grain of sand composed of many prakritic atoms is also composed of many times that number of etheric atoms. The grain of sand is etheric matter as well as prakritic matter. It exists on the etheric plane exactly the same as it exists on the prakritic, and it has etheric form as well as prakritic form.

As each atom of this physical world of ours—whether of land, or water, or air; whether of solid, liquid or gas—is the centre of an etheric molecule, we have two worlds, not one: a physical world and an etheric one; a visible world and an invisible world; a tangible world and an intangible world; a world of effect and a world of cause.

And each animal, including man, is made in the same way. He has a prakritic body and an etheric body; a visible body and an invisible body; an earthly body and one "not made with hands," in common touch with the whole universe.

Chapter Four

What a Teacher Should Teach

Let us suppose that a certain wise teacher of physics places a row of Bunsen burners under a long steel bar having a Daniell's pyrometer at one end, and addresses his class (substantially) as follows:

"At our last lecture we found that the matter of the universe permeated all space, but in two conditions, which we agreed to call physical and etheric, or tangible and intangible. It is all the same matter, subject to the same laws, but differing in the rate of vibration, the physical matter vibrating through one great octave or plane, and the etheric vibrating through another great octave or plane one degree higher—the chording vibration of the matter of the two planes in one note producing what we call energy or force, and with it phenomena.

"This is a bar of steel 36 inches long. It is composed of physical atoms but no two physical atoms touch. Each physical atom is as far apart from every other atom as the stars in heaven from one another—in proportion to their size. The atoms and the spaces between them are so small to our sight that they seem to touch. If we had a microscope of sufficient power to reveal the atom, you would see that no two atoms touch, and that the spaces between them are, as Faraday says, very great in proportion to their size. I showed you last term that what appeared to be a solid stream of water, when magnified and thrown upon a screen, was merely a succession of independent drops that did not touch. I can not yet give you proof of the bar of iron being composed of independent atoms, but that is the fault of our instruments, and you must take my word for it until the proof is simplified and made easy of application.

"Each one of these physical atoms is a miniature world. It is the center of an ocean of ether, composed of many atoms; and while no two physical atoms touch, their etheric atmospheres do touch, and any change in the vibration of the etheric atmosphere of one will be imparted to that of the next. As the vibration of the physical atom must be in harmony with that of its etheric atmosphere, any change coming to one will be imparted to the next, and the next, through the ether surrounding them.

"You can see that the index at the end of the bar has moved, showing that it is now longer. That means the etheric atoms are now vibrating faster, taking more space, and have necessarily forced each physical atom farther apart. The bar is not only longer, but softer, and as the vibrations increase in rapidity the time will come when it will bend by its own weight, and even when it will become a liquid and a gas.

"If you put your hand anywhere near the bar you will feel a sensation called heat, and say it has become hot. The reason for that is that you are in actual and literal touch with the bar or iron through the ether. It is not alone each atom of the bar of iron that is surrounded by the ether, but each atom of the air, and each atom of your body. Their etheric atmospheres are all touching, and the increase in the vibration of the ether surrounding the atoms of iron is imparted to those of the air surrounding it, and these in turn raise the rate of vibration in the etheric atoms surrounding the physical atoms of your hand. This rate of vibration in your nerves causes a sensation, or mental impression, you call "heat." Consciousness of it comes through your sense of touch; but after all it is merely a "rate of vibration" which your brain recognizes and names.

"The bar has now reached a temperature of about 700 degrees, and has become a dull red. Why do you say the color has changed, and why do you say red?

"Because the rate of vibration of the etheric atoms in the bar is now about 412 trillions per second, and this rate of vibration having been imparted to the ether of the air, has in turn been imparted to the ether of your eye, and this rate of vibration in the ether of the nerves of your eye your brain recognizes and calls 'red.'

"The heat still continues and increases. You now have both heat and light. So you see that the ether is not vibrating in a single note, but in two chording notes, producing light and heat. There are two kinds of ether around the iron atom. There is sound also, but the note is too high for one's ears. It is a chord of three notes.

"Professor Silliman, of Yale, discovered over twenty years ago, that the ether could be differentiated into the luminiferous, or light ether, and the sonoriferous, or sound ether.

"Other great scientists since then have found a third ether—the heat ether.

"Their discoveries show that the atmospheric etheric envelope of each etheric atom is made up of etheric atoms of different vibratory powers. As the atmosphere of the earth is made up of atoms of oxygen and nitrogen and argon, so that of an atom is made up of three kinds of ethers, corresponding to three of our senses. That it consists of five ethers, corresponding to our five senses, as the ancient Hindus assert—who can say?

"I mention this subject of the differentiation of the ether merely that you may not suppose that the ether is a simple substance. For the present we will treat it as a simple substance, but next year we will take it up as a compound one.

"This steel bar before you is not one bar, but two bars. There is a visible bar and an invisible bar, the visible bar being made of physical atoms, and the invisible bar of etheric atoms. The etheric bar is invisible, but it is made of matter, the same as the visible bar, and it is just as real, just as truly a bar as the one we see.

"More than this. The etheric, invisible bar is the source and cause of all phenomena connected with the bar. It is the real bar, and the one we see is merely the shadow in physical matter of a real bar. In shape, strength, color, in short, in everything, it depends on the invisible one. The invisible dominates, governs, disposes. The visible is merely its attendant shadow, changing as the invisible, etheric bar changes, and recording for our senses these invisible changes.

"The invisible change always comes first; the invisible phenomena invariably precede the visible.

"In all this physical world—in all this universe—there is nothing, not even a grain of sand or an atom of hydrogen, that is not as this bar of iron is—the shadow cast on a visible world by the unknown and mysterious work of an invisible world.

"Land or water, mountain or lake, man or beast, bird or reptile, cold or heat, light or darkness, all are the reflection in physical matter of the true and real thing in the invisible and intangible world about us. "If we have a visible body we have an invisible one also," said Saint Paul. Modern science has proven he was right, and that it is the invisible body which is the real body.

"If this earth and all that it is composed of—land or ocean or air; man or beast; pyramid or pavement—could be resolved into the physical atoms composing everything in it or on it created by God or man, each atom of this dust would be identical physically. There would not be one kind of atom for iron and another for oxygen.

"The differentiation between what are called elementary substances is first made apparent in the molecule or first combination of the atoms. It is not in the atom itself, unless it be in the size, as may not be improbable. The atoms combine in different numbers to make differently shaped molecules, and it is from this difference in the shape of the molecule that we get the difference between gold and silver, copper and tin, or oxygen and hydrogen.

"In all chemical compounds, such as water and alcohol, the molecules at the base of the two or more substances break up into their original atoms and form a new molecule composed of all the atoms in the two or more things combined. To make this chemical combination we must change the rate of vibration of one or the other or both until they strike a common chord. As we saw last term, oxygen and hydrogen have different specific heats, and no two other elements have the same specific heat, while heat raises the rate of vibration. Any given amount of heat raises the vibration of one more than another. Apply heat, and the rate of one will rise faster than that of the other until they reach a common chord. Then they fall apart and recombine.

"If we pass a current of electricity through this sealed jar containing oxygen and hydrogen in mechanical union, the spark that leaps across the points furnishes the heat, and a drop of water appears and falls to the bottom. A large portion of the gases has disappeared. It has been converted into water. What is left of the gases will expand and fill the bottle.

"The drop of water but for local causes, but for a certain attraction of the earth, would float in the centre of the jar at the centre of gravity, as the earth does in space. But the centre of gravity of the two bodies is far within the earth, and the drop gets as close to it as it can. The earth's 'pull' takes it to the bottom. If the jar were far enough away in space the drop would float, as the earth floats, at a point where all pulls balance, and the drop of water would have enough pull of its own, enough gravity within itself to hold all the gas left in the jar to itself as an atmosphere. It would be a centre of energy, a minature world.

"The drop of water is not a homogenous mass. About one third of the bulk of the drop of water is made up of independent oxygen and hydrogen atoms interspersed through it, as any liquid is through this piece of blotting paper. And it has, and keeps, by its own attraction, an atmosphere of the gas. Each molecule of water has a thin layer, or skin, of the gas; even as it comes from this faucet.

"Let us return again to the physical dust, the atom. Why should it form by fives for iron, by nines for hydrogen? Where did the atom come from? What is it? We know that like the drop of water, it is a miniature world with an atmosphere of ether; and the natural inference is that it is made from ether as the drop of water was made from gas. Many things confirm this inference, and it may be accepted as 'a working hypothesis' that it is made from ether as the drop of water is made from gas, by the chemical union of a large amount of ether of different kinds, the etheric molecules of which consist of 2 and 3 or 5 and 4 etheric atoms, and that the tendency to combine in this or that number in physical matter is an inherited tendency brought with it from the etheric world of matter on which, or in which, each element of this world is two or more. There is no kind of matter in this physical world, that has not its prototype in the etheric, and the laws of its action and reaction here are laws which it inherits and brings with it. They are not laws made here. They are laws of the other world—even as the matter itself is matter of the other world.

> "In 1882, Professor Lodge, in a lecture before the Royal Institution on 'The Luminiferous Ether' defined it as:

"'One continuous substance, filling all space, which can vibrate as light, which can be sheared into positive and negative electricity, which in whirls constitutes matter, and which transmits by continuity and not impact every action and reaction of which matter is capable.'

"This reads today like baby-talk but at that time (eighteen years ago), it was considered by many timid conservative scientists as 'a daring movement.' It is noteworthy in that it was the first public scientific announcement that the physical matter is a manifestation or form of the ether. And it was made before general acceptance of the division of the ether into soniferous, luminiferous and tangiferous.

"'Which in whirls constitutes matter.' Professor Lodge believed that 'some etheric molecules revolved so rapidly on their axis that they could not be penetrated.' Watch the soap-bubbles that I am blowing. Each and every one is revolving as the earth revolves, from west to east. What I wish to call your attention to is the fact that can be proven, both mathematically and theoretically, that at a certain rate of speed in the revolution they could not be penetrated by any rifle-ball. At a higher rate of speed they would be harder than globes of solid chilled steel, harder even than carbon. Professor Lodge believed that the etheric molecule revolved so rapidly that, thin as it was in its shell, it gave us the dust out of which worlds were made. There is one fatal error in this idea, although it is held even now by many. It is based entirely on gravity, and gravity is alone considered in its problems. There are two great forces in the universe, not one, as many scientific people fail to remember —Gravity and Apergy, or the centrifugal and centripetal forces. The pull in is and must be always balanced by the pull out. There is in the universe as much repulsion as attraction, and the former is a force quite as important as the latter. The bubble's speed kept increasing until apergy, the tendency to fly off, overcame gravity, and it ruptured.

"Professor Lodge failed to take into account this apergic force, this tendency to fly off, when he gave such high revolutionary speed to the etheric molecules, a speed in which apergy would necessarily exceed gravity. The failure to take apergy into consideration has been the undoing of many physicists.

"Today we know that the ether is matter, the same as our own, only finer and rarer and in much more rapid vibration. We know that this ether has its solids, liquids and gases formed from molecules of its atoms, even as our own are formed. We know that its atoms combine as ours do, and while we have but eighty elementary combinations, it must have more than double the number. We know that every form and shape and combination of these elements from this plane flows from inherited tendencies having their root in the etheric world.

"The two worlds are one world—as much at one with ours as the world of gas about us is at one with our liquids and solids. It is 'continuity, not impact.' They not only touch everywhere and in everything, but they are one and the same in action and reaction."

Thus spake a certain wise teacher of physics. To his wise utterances, we can only add that such as we are today "we see through a glass, darkly." Yet there will come a day when the physical bandages will be removed from our eyes, and we shall see face to face the beauty and grandeur and glory of this invisible world, and that in truth it 'transmits by continuity and not impact every action and reaction of which matter is capable,' forming one continuous chain of cause and effect, without a link missing. There are no gulfs to cross; no bridges to be made. It is here; not there. It is at one with us. And we are at one with it. One and the same law controls and guides the etheric atom and the physical atom made from its molecules, whether the latter are made in "whirls," as at first supposed, or by orderly combination as now believed.

In fact, this visible world of ours is the perfect product of the other invisible one, having in it its root and foundation, the very sap of its life.

Chapter Five

The Four Manifested Planes

The oriental idea of the universe does not differ fundamentally in its general conception, from that of modern science, but it goes farther and explains more. The physics of the secret doctrine are based upon a material universe of four planes of vibration and a spiritual universe of three planes of vibration beyond matter. This Something in vibration may be given the English name, Consciousness—without entering upon its nature.

Spirit is consciousness in vibration and undifferentiated.

Matter is consciousness in vibration and differentiated.

As we divide the seven octaves of a piano into Treble and Bass for clearness of thought and writing, so the Hidden Knowledge divides the seven octaves of vibration, or planes, into Spirit and Matter. In their ultimate analysis they are one and the same thing, as ice and water are the same thing; but for study they must be differentiated.

The material and physical universe consists of four planes of matter, or four great octaves of vibration, each differentiated from the other as in our physics prakriti is differentiated from ether. The material universe, the ancient physics teach, was originally pure thought, Manasa, the product of the spiritual planes above. This manasic world was differentiated, a real world. That is to say it was given elementary substances by the union of its atoms in different sized molecules. Some of its elements combined and formed Prana. The prana gathered and formed other worlds, pranic worlds. Then in the pranic world etheric worlds were formed; and finally in the etheric worlds, prakritic globes like the earth were formed. The earth is the centre of a prakritic globe, revolving in ether around the sun. The sun is the centre of a solar globe of ether, revolving in prana around Alcyone. Alcyone is the centre of a stellar globe of prana revolving in manasa around the central and hidden sun of the great manasic globe. These four conditions of matter prakriti, ether, prana, and manasa are the earth, water, fire, air of the Ancient Metaphysics, the four elements of matter, and are present in every atom of prakriti. When the atom of prana was formed, it had an envelope of manasa. When the atom of ether was formed it had an envelope of pranic-manasic atoms. When the prakritic atom was formed it had an envelope of etheric-pranic- manasic atoms, each of its encircling etheric atoms being the centre of a pranic molecule, and each pranic atom of that molecule being the centre of a manasic molecule.

Each atom of prakriti was the material universe in miniature. It held the potentialities of mind, life, and phenomena. In every aggregation of atoms, there were the four planes, each in touch through the Cosmic Mind, its manasa, with other atoms in the universe, with every other globe of whatever kind. "As above, so below," was the secret Key-word. The unity of all the material universe in its prakriti, ether, prana and manasa, was the corner stone of this knowledge. The three planes above prakriti were called Astral, and in common speech there was the ordinary division into two planes, visible and invisible, or "Spirit," as the invisible was called, and "Matter," as the visible was called. Only in the hidden secret doctrine of physics, and in the open metaphysics which were a "stumbling block" and "foolishness" to those who had not the "inner light" of the physics, were the three divisions of the "astral" made known, and the true distinction between the spirit of the three higher planes and the matter of the four lower was kept out of the metaphysics, or only vaguely alluded to.

There is no "oriental science" because the oriental does not attach the same value to merely physical knowledge that we do. But that must not be understood to imply that there is no oriental physics. In all the matters that interest us now, as far as principles are concerned, the oriental knew all that we know. He knew it thousands of years ago, when our ancestors were sleeping with the cave bears.

"That is all the good it did him," the scientist says. No. That is not true. It is perfectly true that the oriental, the Babylonian who carved on the Black Stone now in the British Museum the five moons of Jupiter, exposing himself to the derision of our astronomers prior to their own discovery of the fifth moon in 1898, did not care particularly whether there were four moons or five, and had no sale for any telescopes he might make, for no one else cared particularly. But it was not true that he did not care for any and all knowledge that would improve his spiritual condition by giving him correct ideas of the universe and of his own part in it. To him life was more than meat and the body more than raiment. He was more afraid of sin than of ignorance. We are more afraid of ignorance than of sin. He preferred to better men's moral condition; we prefer to better their physical condition.

If one of the Sages of the East could be called up and put on the stand to be questioned, he would say, substantially:

"You are right in regard to your ether, and to prakriti being ether that has been dropped a great octave in vibration. Your physical atom is surrounded by a molecule of ether, this molecule containing many atoms of ether. The chording vibration does produce all physical phenomena.

"But where did the ether atom come from? How can you explain how and whence life comes, or what it is? This explains physical, but how do you explain vital phenomena?

"You are wrong in assuming that all the matter of the universe apart from the earth or planets is ether and only ether. The etheric world in which you are interested ends with your solar system. It ends with each solar system, to the people of that system. Between each solar system and another there is another form of matter that is not ether.

"This etheric solar world of ours is very large, many billions of miles in diameter; but it is not the whole universe. You know that the sun and all its planets are revolving around the star Alcyone. Your astronomers told you that years ago, and they have recently given you the rate of speed as 4,838 miles per hour.

"Did you not see and know that if they had this revolution around a central sun it must be within a solar globe?

"Did you think that the sun and its planets, and other suns and their planets, were tearing their way through the ether like so many fish on a dipsy-hook from a Marblehead fishing smack running before the wind?

"Did it never occur to you that the ether of this solar system must be revolving around this central sun? The whole solar system, ether and planets, are revolving around Alcyone, and the reason why their minor revolution around the sun is not affected by it is because the solar system is a vast globe of ether, having a thinner and rarer medium to revolve in, the same as our earth has. It is the motion of a fly in a moving car.

"Now fix your attention on this globe of ether, this solar globe. You must do it to get the concept before you. You have known of it all your life without once really apprehending it, for you have never learned to think, or to utilize the knowledge that was given you. The idea is as new and as strange as if you had never known it.

"What lies beyond the surface of the solar globe? Something must; something as much rarer and thinner than the ether as the ether is rarer and thinner than prakriti. Can you not guess?

"It is Prana, the life force of the universe. As prakriti is made from ether, so ether is made from prana. It is made in the same way. Each atom of the ether is the centre of a molecule of prana, surrounded by an atmosphere of pranic atoms, exactly as your prakritic atom is surrounded by an atmosphere of etheric atoms. You say that each atom of prakriti is the centre of a molecule of ether. So it is. But each atom of that etheric molecule is the centre of a pranic molecule. Each atom of your physical matter is triple, not double.

"You say that all physical phenomena come from the chording vibration of the etheric and prakritic atoms of the two planes of matter. Yes. But do you not see that all vital phenomena come from the chording vibration of the pranic, etheric, and prakritic atom of the three planes of matter which are in each atom?

"In the living leaf the three planes are sounding in chord in each atom of it. In the dead leaf, drying up and falling to pieces, only the lower two are sounding in chord. The silver chord has been broken.

"Each atom of prakriti you say has the potentiality of some kind of phenomenon. We add 'and of life also.' The potentialities of life are in every atom of prakriti. Even the atom of iron may live in the blood. It cannot become a part of any living organism until its prana is sounding the chord of life in unison with the ether and prakriti—the threefold silver chord.

"What is the centre of this prana? It is Alcyone. There are other solar globes beside ours circling around Alcyone, and we have been considering only our own solar globe of ether. Alcyone is the centre of the prana in which they revolve as the sun is the centre of our ether in which the planets revolve. As this prana has a centre around which we revolve with other solar systems, then it must have a center of gravity.

"Then this prana is a globe.

"The prana does not then fill this material universe. There must be yet another form of matter rarer and finer than prana, from which prana is made, as ether is made from prana and prakriti from ether. Have we any other class of phenomena to explain, except vital and physical? Yes, there is a very important class, mental. And here we have the explanation, if we exercise our reason.

"These pranic globes are floating in an ocean of manasa, matter in its rarest form.

"Each atom of prana is formed from manasa, exactly as ether was formed from prana, and each pranic atom in the universe is the centre of a manasic molecule, having an atmosphere of manasic atoms.

"So we are not exact in giving the prakritic atom three planes or octaves of vibration. It has four. You merely surround it with etheric atoms, and this is correct so far as it goes. You only wish to explain physical problems. But there are other problems to be explained, problems of life and mind, and the same knowledge you have explains them as well as the others, if you simply avail yourself of it. That you do not consider the atom as four-fold instead of two-fold is your own fault. I have not told you anything you did not already know. I have only asked you to apply your present knowledge of physics to these problems of life and mind, and apply your reasoning powers.

"The chording vibration in an atom of matter of

"The two planes produces Force, or phenomena

"The three planes produces Life—the silver chord

"The four planes produces Mind—the golden chord.

"You say there is no gulf between the prakritic and etheric worlds; that it is one continuous world; and all its phenomena are by continuity and not impact. That is true, but it is not the whole truth.

"There is no gulf to cross between the prakritic and etheric worlds; none to cross between that and the manasic. The four worlds are one great world, continuous, interchangeable. Through the four as well as through the two, there is continuity and not impact. Whether it is an atom or a world, the four are there. Nothing, no combination of atoms, no matter of any kind, however small or large, can exist in this prakritic world unless it has the four elements, which from time immemorial our philosophers have called Earth, Water, Fire, Air, meaning the four globes or forms of matter in the universe. We do not have to leave the earth to live in the etheric globe. It is here. Nor do we have to go millions of miles to reach the pranic globe. It is here. The problems of light and heat are no easier than the problems of birth and death. The pranic globe is within us; within everything. So is the manasic.

"It is here on these higher planes that the chances for worthy study are greatest. At least we think so, though you may not. We live on the manasic—pranic—etheric globe on precisely the same terms that we live on this of prakriti, and the problems of the three are equally open to us.

"If there are any who care to follow up the line of thought I have opened, who care for the questions that interest us of the East, I will talk as long as they care to listen, provided they will not ask for knowledge that will give them power over others, which cannot fail to be used for evil."

This is but a glimpse of Hindu physics, yet it has helped us in the metaphysics. We now understand the chain of globes—in part. The earth is fourfold. As each atom of the earth is fourfold, so their aggregations give us prakritic earth, an etheric earth, a pranic earth, and a manasic earth—in coadunition and not like the skin of an onion. They are separate and distinct globes, each on its own plane. It is four down and three up for the Angel entering matter, whether from the outmost boundary of manasic matter, or the surface of the earth, or the cover of a baseball. The "chain of globes" in the Secret Doctrine represents the unity of the material universe.

The three-fold nature of the astral model is revealed, and the unity of all prakritic things. But more than that, to many minds, will be the explanation it gives of why there are but four planes of vibration in matter; that the highest form of development in prakriti shows only four elements, prakriti or body, sensation or force, life, and mind, and that these last three, present in all things in esse, become present in posse when they work together harmonically.

Chapter Six

Our Place on Earth

The next time our wise man from the east was asked to "say a few words and make his own topic," he spoke, perhaps, as follows:

"How large do you think the earth is? You answer promptly, 7,912 miles in diameter. You are as far out of the way as you were in supposing that our sun could be a centre of gravity of a lot of planets revolving around it and around Alcyone without being a globe of ether. Now that it has been mentioned, you see very clearly for yourself that it must be a solar globe of ether. It follows from one of your physical axioms. When I tell you why the earth is and must be about fifty thousand miles in diameter, you will see that it must be so, and that you knew it all the time, but never stopped to formulate your knowledge. You have had the knowledge for three centuries without applying it.

"It was in 1609 that your greatest astronomer, John Kepler, announced as one of three harmonic laws by which the universe was governed, that the squares of the times of the planets were proportional to the cubes of their distances from the sun; and that this law was true in physics and everywhere. No one of your scientists has had the wisdom to study out what it meant, and for three centuries, for 291 years, you have repeated his words like so many parrots, instead of using the key he gave you to unlock the mysteries of the universe. A corollary of his law is that the planets move in their orbits because they are impelled thereto between the two forces, and move in a mean curve between them; but it was not until 1896 that you discovered that the mean between two forces is always a curve and never a straight line. You have not a text book in a school today that does not repeat this fundamental and absurd error—which you have known for three centuries to be an error—that the motion resulting from a mean between forces is "in a straight line." The curves resulting here are not to be measured easily, and are so large that small segments appear straight lines; and it was not until Carpenter demonstrated it mathematically that any one could believe it true.

"There are two great forces in this universe. Your grandfathers called them Centripetal and Centrifugal forces; your fathers called them Gravity and Apergy, names which still cling to them; and you call them Attraction and Repulsion.

"It was Kepler, not Newton, who discovered that Attraction or Gravity was in inverse proportion to the square of the distance.

"You know the meaning of this mystic phrase, 'as the squares of the distance.' You understand that it means the attraction at two feet is only one-fourth the attraction at one foot; at four feet only one-sixteenth; at eight feet, only one sixty-fourth.

"But who knows or cares for Kepler's great law of Repulsion, or Apergy? That was that the 'square of the times are as the cubes of the distance.' It has lain fallow for centuries. No one of your western physicists has ever studied it, or tried to explain it. It remains just where Kepler left it, as the mere law of orbital revolution of the planets only.

"It is the key to the proper understanding of the universe.

"'The squares of the times are as the cubes of the distance' means that all motion is the result of two forces acting upon prakriti, and that where the two forces are balanced, or equal, the result in motion is a circle or ellipse, the square of the Repulsion being equal to the cube of the Attraction to make them equal and produce a circle. In other cases they produce hyperbola and parabola.

"This is a little dry—nearly all fundamental knowledge is—but the reward of patience is great.

"The orbital speed of the earth is about 60,000 miles per hour. The attraction of the sun exactly equals the repulsion created by the motion; more accurately, the speed created by the repulsion. The result of the two forces working together at exact balance is a circle. An ellipse is a circle bent a little, and the ellipse in which the earth actually moves comes from varying attraction and repulsion. Kepler's second law covers that.

"If the orbital speed of the earth were a mile less per hour, or even a foot less, then the earth would wind up around the sun as a dog gets wound up with his chain around a tree. If this speed were a mile more per hour, then the earth would wind out, each year getting farther and farther away, until finally it would be lost. When the speed is exactly proportional to the pull—that is, when it is as 1.6 is to 2,—the result is a circular orbit, the eccentricity of which is caused by certain fluctuations in the attraction and repulsion.

"Suppose a planet were to be placed so that it would have a time of two years. Its distance from the sun would be 1.6 that of the earth. Why? Because to get the time doubled we would have to take the square root of 4; and to get the distance the cube root of the same number, 4. If you wish to be very exact the cube root is 1.5889, but 1.6 is near enough for all ordinary work.

"If you wanted to find out the distance of a planet revolving in six months you would divide the earth's distance by 1.6.

"In proportion you get any time or distance you may desire with absolute accuracy. The distance of any planet from the sun gives its time, or its time gives its distance—when that of any of the others is known. This law applies throughout the universe; in everything and everywhere. It is not a law of orbital revolution alone, but a law of all motion.

"Our moon has a time of 29 days and a speed of about 50,000 miles per day. If the speed were greater it would leave us, if less it would wind up, falling to the earth in the form of a spiral.

"At what distance would it have to be to have a time of fourteen days? Divide 240,000 miles by 1.6. A seven-day moon, would be 1.6 that distance. And the exact distance for a one-day moon, for a moon that would always be in the same place in the heavens, moving as the earth revolved on its axis, would be about 24,998 miles.

"This gives us the line of 24-hour axial rotation, the true surface of the earth, and the sheer-line of prakritic matter. Beyond that line is the ether; within that line is prakriti.

"It is the line of no weight, where gravity and apergy exactly balance. Inside that line gravity exceeds apergy and everything revolving in less time, or that time, must fall to the centre. It is the true surface of any 24-hour globe of this size and weight. A moon to revolve around the earth in less than one day must move faster than the earth to develop enough apergy to overcome the attraction. That phenomenon we see in the moons of Mars, which are within its atmosphere; within the planet itself.

"We of the East learned this true size of the earth over six thousand years ago, from observing the moons of Jupiter. The times of the first three are doubled. We asked ourselves what this meant and found that their distance was increased by the cube root of 4 when their times were increased by the square root of 4; that time was to distance as 1.6 was to 2. Then we applied the key, and found it unlocked many mysteries.

"The first lesson this taught us was that we did not live on the earth, but within the earth, at the line of liquid and gaseous changes, where the three forms of matter meet and mingle and interchange with each other. We lived at the bottom of a gaseous ocean 21,000 miles above us, and 4,000 miles from the centre of the globe. It gave us an entirely new conception of the earth, and of our place in it.

"We saw that we lived in a narrow belt, or skin, of the earth, not more than 100 miles thick, perhaps not more than ten miles. Within this belt the prakritic elementary substances varied their condition, combined, and made forms by increasing or decreasing vibration. It was the creative and destructive zone, the evolutionary "mother"—the liquid level of the prakriti—the seat of all physical phenomena. Fifty miles above, the masses of nitrogen and oxygen and argon were too cold to change their rate of vibration. Fifty miles below the surface of the earth all things were too hot for changes in vibration. In this kinetic belt, between two static masses our bodies had been made, and also, in all probability, all combinations of the elementary substances. It was four thousand miles to the centre of the static prakritic mass beneath us; twenty-one thousand miles to the surface of the static prakritic mass above us, and the small kinetic belt between was only one hundred miles thick. But we had one consolation, the prakriti we had was all kinetic, and the best in the whole mass.

"The second lesson it taught us was that as the earth had been made in the etheric globe, in a corresponding skin or plane of kinetic etheric energy, with our ether the best of the solar output, that we ourselves were subject through our ether to the phenomena of that kinetic solar plane in precisely the same way we now are to the phenomena of the kinetic prakritic plane. Once rid of the fallacious notion that we were creatures of the surface of the earth, once clearly conscious that we were creatures of the interior, of the bottom of this gaseous ocean, then we could understand not only how the earth could be created in this etheric globe, but how we could be creatures of the solar globe living on it.

"When we learned that lesson, and learned it well, it dawned upon us that we were living in the pranic globe at the same kinetic level or plane of that globe, the line where its solids and liquids and gases mingled and passed from one state to another, the kinetic belt in which our solar globe has been made, and that we were living as truly on that globe as we were on this prakritic globe. Our position on each globe was the same.

"And then the great truth came that we lived in the manasic globe, at the same kinetic level; and that we lived our lives on the four globes simultaneously. Our bodies are fourfold. Every atom is fourfold, ready to respond in our minds to the vibrations of the Manasic world, in our vitality to the pranic vibrations of the pranic world, in our nerves to the etheric vibrations of the etheric world, and in our prakriti to vibrations of the prakritic world. Each one of our bodies lived on its own earth globe, for there were four globes of this earth—in coadunition—in its corresponding kind of globe.

"The four earth globes became one globe, as our four bodies were one body; and the chain of four kinds of globes in matter became one globe, as the manasic with the others on it.

"These four kinds of globes were the beginning and the end of matter, as we distinguish and know matter. They were not the end of vibration; or of planes of vibration; or of realms beyond this material universe; but they were the limits of all that is common to each and every atom of this lower plane of vibration.

"It is upon this solid and perfect foundation of physics, that accounts for and explains every kind of phenomena, we have constructed our metaphysics. All that belongs to these four lower planes we consider and treat as physics. All that relates to the planes beyond we consider metaphysics. Can you teach a child equation of payments before he knows the first four rules? You would not attempt such a task. The first four rules are the physics of arithmetic; all beyond is the metaphysics of arithmetic. It flows out of them. Can you comprehend our system of metaphysics until you have clearly and completely mastered our physics? Would you not get into a fog at the very start?

"There can be no system of metaphysics without a solid foundation of physics. The idea is unthinkable. The one grows out of the other. It is its life; its fruit, its flower.

"You have no western system of physics. Your physics are without form and void; patchwork, constantly changing. There is no substantial foundation for any system of metaphysics. What you say or do in physics is fragmentary or chaotic.

"It is perfectly true, so far as you have gone through the first invisible world of ether, you are much more masters of detail than we are.

"We have not cared particularly for the minor details by which explosives are made, or metals obtained from oxides. We have preferred to push on into realms beyond as fast as we could, seeking first the Kingdom of Heaven and its Righteousness, knowing that when it was found all these things would be added unto us."

Chapter Seven

The Four Globes

That we live in the earth, not on the earth, is one of the most important of the facts of eastern physics in the study of its metaphysics. The mathematical and physical proof that the physical earth is 50,000 miles in diameter should not be passed over lightly in our haste to get on, for the perfect understanding of all this fact implies makes easy the comprehension of how we live etherically in the solar etheric globe, of how we live pranically in the stellar pranic globe, and how we live manasically in the manasic globe.

As we live within the narrow "skin" of phenomena, not more than 100 miles thick, of this prakritic globe, with the whole earth within the corresponding skin of phenomena of the solar etheric globe, within the kinetic belt in which it was made, the ether which surrounds each prakritic molecule is not merely any and every kind of ether, but that particular kind of kinetic ether, which, by changing its rate of vibration through an octave, creates phenomena. The ether of all prakritic matter belongs to the kinetic or creative belt of the solar etheric globe. It is not static ether. The ether in our prakriti is in touch with all the prakritic kinetic ether of the solar globe, subject to all solar laws of change; and all our prak-solar laws of change; and all our prakritic matter, a mere detail of it, is a part of the solar phenomena. "Our father, the sun," or "Dyaus pitar" ("heavenly father"—Latin, Jupiter) meant more once than it does now. Then the solar globe was the first heaven, and to live under its laws, puttings off the coat of skin, was an object which men believed to be worth striving for. They recognized, as we do not, that our prakritic laws were not all they had to obey; that the higher law of the solar globe on which they lived, of which the lower prakritic laws were merely an outcome and detail, was worthy of the closest study. And they recognized that these higher laws of the etheric globe were metaphysical as well as physical; that our moral law flows out of the moral law of the solar etheric world, as our physics flow from and out of solar physics. Religion is correct in its assumption of this higher law of morals; incorrect only in its grasp and explanation. Science is correct in holding only in its assumption that it is physical science; incorrect only in its assumption that it is physical science of this plane and globe only. There is no quarrel between science and religion when the full knowledge of one stands beside the full knowledge of the other. They are twin-sisters.

This solar-etheric globe in which we are interested revolves around Alcyone within that kinetic belt or skin of prana which is subject to phenomena or vibration through one octave—else it would never have been formed. All prana in the solar-etheric globe is of this particular kind of kinetic prana, which creates life of all kinds—which is subject to vibration through one octave. The solar globe is a detail of kinetic prana only, one of its phenomena. Necessarily, all our prana is of this kinetic kind, and our earth a minor detail of it in the Alcyone globe. All the changes and combinations possible in kinetic prana on the pranic globe are possible here, in our kinetic prana, as all the phenomena of the etheric world are possible here in our kinetic ether.

As our earth is a globe of ether and a globe of prana as well as a globe of prakriti; we are actually living on a small "cabbage" of that pranic globe, and subject to all its laws.

In the vast manasic globe that includes this whole material universe there is the same kinetic belt or skin of "phenomena" or vibration similar to that kinetic belt in which we live on the earth, and the manasa which permeates the Alcyonic globe, the solar globe, and the earth is that kinetic manasa which is involving and evolving. This involving and evolving kinetic manasa of the Alcyonic globe is that which surrounds every atom of ether of the solar globe and every atom of prakriti of this earth globe. In the great manasic globe this earth of ours is a minute village of Helios (sun) county, in the state of Alcyone. We are actually and literally living in this manasic globe precisely as we live in this earth, and as in the village we are subject to all the laws of the manasic world, we can study them here in this village as well as we could elsewhere. We can study them as easily as we study our prakritic village laws, or our etheric county laws, for all the forms of manasa subject to them anywhere are here with us. We are not limited to a study of the prakritic laws of the village fathers, nor yet to the etheric laws of the supervisors of Helios county, as scientists say, nor even to the state laws of Alcyone; only the manasic laws of the Universe limit our material studies in that direction. As some men on this earth never leave their native village and never know or care for any matters outside of it, so in this little earth village, in the kinetic belt of the manasic globe, there are men who do not care to know anything which relate to matters outside its boundaries. As some men may pass the boundaries of their village, but not of their county, caring only for the matters concerning it, so the western scientists of this earth village on the manasic globe do not pass the boundaries of Helios county, caring only for etheric matters. The philosophers and wise men of the East are broader minded and from time immemorial have taken greater interest in the pranic affairs of Alcyone and the manasic condition of the universe in which Alcyone is a state than in the rustic murmur of their village or the gossip of their county.

There is nothing lacking in our manasic earth-village, nothing that is in more abundant measure in our county, state, and nation. We are of the best.

We of this village may imagine, if we like, that there is nothing beyond the village limits, and nothing in it but that which relates to the village. We have the right to be silly, if we wish to be. And it is no sign of wisdom to say that there is a county beyond, but that the county boundaries end all, and only village and county politics may be studied. The European who believed—no Asiatic or African or American could have believed — that the earth rested on an elephant and the elephant on a turtle was wise, in comparison. Nor is it any sign of intelligence to say that we may learn something of the village and county while we live, but that to learn anything about the state and nation we must wait until we are dead. There are too many in the village who are familiar with both state and nation, and who have studied their laws, for this to be anything but idiotic.

Chapter Eight

The Battle Ground

Each and every one of our eighty-odd elementary substances owe their condition—whether solid, liquid, or gas—to their rate of vibration. We have reduced all gases to a liquid and nearly all to a solid form. Conversely, we have raised all solids to a liquid and nearly all to a gaseous condition. This has been done by reducing or raising the vibration of each within one octave—each one of the eighty odd having a special octave, a tone or half-tone different from any other. Normally, the solids, vibrating in the lower notes, gather together under Attraction; while the gases, vibrating in the higher notes, diffuse under Repulsion. Between them, created by the interchange of these two forces, is our "skin" of phenomena, or kinetics.

Broadly, the attraction of the universe comes from its vibration at certain centres in the three higher notes; the repulsion comes from its vibration everywhere else in the three higher notes. The central note, D of the scale, represents the battle ground between the field of kinetics. This in simple illustration is water turning into gas.

This is the great battle ground, the only one worth considering in a general view. There are minor "critical stages" which the chemist studies, but for us, in this broad sketch of the universe, the important battle-ground is that between solid and liquid on one side representing gravity, and gas on the other, representing apergy.

All the solids and liquids of this earth of ours gather at the centre, in a core, each of the elements (or their combinations) in this core vibrating in their three lower notes, producing the attraction, which is "in proportion to the mass" and which decreases from the surface of the core "as the square of the substance."

Around this central core gather all the elements vibrating in the three higher notes of their octave as gases, producing repulsion which increases by 1.6 for each doubled time. It is worth while making this clear. It has never before appeared in print.

Let the amount of apergy, or repulsion, or centrifugal force at the surface of the earth be represented by x. This is the result of motion at the rate of 1,000 miles per hour. Make this motion 2,000 miles per hour, and the apergy is increased 1.6. Four thousand miles above the surface of this earth the rotation is at the rate of 2,000. It is the globe of 48,000 miles in circumference revolving in 24 hours, and the speed is doubled. This apergy has increased by 1.6. As the apergy increases at this rate every time the speed is doubled, at a distance of 21,000 miles the speed is 7,000 miles per hour and the centrifugal force has been increased nearly four times what it was at the surface of the ocean. The attraction has been decreased to about one-thirtieth. At the surface it is equal to 120 x. At 4,000 miles to one-quarter, or 30 x; at 16,000 miles to one-sixteenth, or 7 x; and at 21,000 miles to 4 x.

If "equatorial gravity is about 120 times that of the equatorial apergy," at the ocean level, then at the distance of 21,000 miles from it, in a revolving globe, the two forces would be equal; the "pull" of each being 4 x, and an anchor will weigh no more than a feather, for weight is the excess of gravity or apergy.

If the pyramids had been built of the heaviest known material on the gases 21,000 miles above us, and so that they should revolve in the same time, 7,000 miles per hour, they would remain there. All the attraction of the solid core of the earth that could be exerted on them at that distance would not be enough to pull them an inch nearer to it through our gaseous envelope. Their gaseous foundation there would be as firm as igneous rock here.

The force of repulsion created by the three higher notes of an octave means just as much at the attraction created by the three lower notes, whether it is in a chemical retort, within this earth, or within this universe. The two forces balance, and are exactly equal. They fight only within kinetic zones.

Given the vast manasic globe of differentiated matter, its atoms uniting in different numbers to form molecules as the bases of elementary substances, manasic substances, of course. The thrill of vibration is sweeping through it from the spiritual plane above, and the elements (and their combinations) which answer in the lower notes gather and form a core, the Invisible Central Sun, with its attraction. The elements answering in the higher notes gather around it with their repulsion. So the two opposing forces were born, with a vast kinetic skin for a battle-ground between them.

The attraction of the invisible central sun manifests itself to us in prakriti as Light. The repulsion of its covering, or the higher static vibration of manasa, manifests itself to us as Darkness. The first creative act in or on matter was the creation of Light and its separation from the Darkness. The next creative act was the establishment of a kinetic skin or zone between them, a firmament in which the two forces of Light and Darkness could strive for mastery. "And God called the firmament Heaven." The third creative act was the gathering of the solids and liquids together, and the beginning of the kinetic work in the creation of forms and shapes, by the cross play of the two forces in their combinations of solid with gases.

All this had to happen before the manasa combined and dropped in vibration to prana—and before the pranic globes were formed and the Light could be manifested to us through them. It may be well to read the first chapter of Genesis over and ask forgiveness for our ignorance, from the writer who records this creation of the pranic globes as the fourth act of creation, and the creation of the etheric sun and prakritic moon to follow that. That record is mutilated, fragmentary; but the writer of it knew the facts. If we had the full story, instead of a sentence here and there, taken from an older story not to tell of creation but to hide another tale for the priest, the writer of Genesis would laugh last.

But let us return to the kinetic skin of energy between Light and the Darkness—the firmament which God calls Heaven—the battle ground for gravity and apergy, or attraction and repulsion, or good and evil, or the powers of light and darkness. This skin is like that of an onion, thickest at the equator and thinnest at the poles—not only on this earth but in the solar, alcyonic, and manasic globes. The equatorial belt, where phenomena are richest in the manasic globes, we call the Milky Way; in the solar globe we call it the plane of the ecliptic; and on the earth, the tropics. Modern science has not yet found it in Alcyonic globe—because it has never thought of looking for it.

This division of the Light from the Darkness was all that was required for evolution on the manasic globe within the kinetic belt. This evolution was not confined to the making of a few alcyonic or pranic globes. It was (and is) a great and wonderful evolution beyond words and almost beyond imagination. It is the Heaven which mankind has longed to see and know. The writer of Genesis mixed it with the creation of this earth, using earthly metaphors. Before finding fault, we should better his language. We have not the words in physics to do it, and must wait for our metaphysics. But of one thing we may be sure, that the pranic- alcyonic globes here and there at the "sea level" of the manasic globe—in what God calls Heaven—amount to no more on that globe, or in Heaven, than so many balls of thistle-down blown across a meadow do on this earth of ours. Everything that can be created in thought must be there. It is in thought only, but in thought it is differentiated as sharply as anything in prakriti. The manasic world, the Heaven of the Bible, is as real as our own world can possibly be; in fact, more real, for when ours is resolved back into its final elements, it will be but "the dust of the ground" of the manasic world.

The pranic globes created in this manasic skin by Sound, or the Logos, or vibration, evolved in identically the same way—with a central static core and an outer static envelope, of low and high vibration in prana, creating attraction and repulsion, or gravity and apergy. The kinetic skin between, in which these forces play in the pranic world, makes a real, not an imaginary pranic world, though but a faint reflection of the manasic. When our father, the Central Invisible Sun, transfers his attraction to these alcyonic suns, the Light has something in which to manifest itself, and we "see" this manifesting core and call it Alcyone, and its manifestation Light; but light in its last material analysis is but the static mind or thought vibrating in the three lower notes of the octave.

Chapter Nine

The Dual Man

Within the alcyonic globes of differentiated pranic-manasic atoms the vibration divided them also into solid-liquid cores and gaseous envelopes, and a kinetic skin of phenomena. And then a new world—a world of Life, came into material existence. All the atoms of thought or manasa, surrounding each and every pranic atom, and making its molecule of energy, so to speak, were that particular kind of kinetic manasa ready to change its rate of vibration within an octave, and the forms prana assumes from the action of thought within the kinetic belt were living and thinking. Each pranic globe, which was a small state of product of the manasic, consisted of two globes in coadunition—two in one. Each pranic atom was the centre of a manasic molecule and represented the universe. All things were two in one, created by harmonic vibration between them, and existence by the greater strength of the lower notes, or attraction. It was at once less and more wonderful than the manasic world—a specialized form of it.

When within this kinetic belt of the prana the etheric solar globes formed here and there, they were three fold, each atom of the new plane of matter having its surrounding envelope of prana- manasa—a specialization of the pranic world in which (what we call) force had been added to life and mind. The static ether, vibrating in each of its elements through one octave, divided into central core (our sun, and other suns) and outer covering, with a skin or belt of kinetic energy, "as above" which developed an etheric world. All things on this etheric world were caused by the harmonic vibration between the etheric atoms and their surrounding envelopes, except that while all things in this etheric world must have life, not all need have mind. The chord of three was not necessary to create; the chord of two was enough, and the manasic atoms might cease to vibrate in chord with the prana and ether without affecting the creation. Only in the etheric world (and below it) could there be living mindless ones. To the etheric globes the stellar pranic cores transferred their light, which manifested itself in the solid static ether as Attraction and in the gaseous static ether as Repulsion, within the kinetic skin of each etheric world more specialized and less varied than the pranic.

Our sun is not of prakriti, but of static ether, composed of the separate and individual elementary substances of the ether, and their compounds vibrating in the lower notes of their octaves. It is our father, not our elder brother. Its envelope of static ether in which the planet revolves is composed of the elementary substances and combinations vibrating in the higher notes of their octave. The light transferred to this etheric globe from its mother, Alcyone, manifests itself in the lower vibration of the sun as Attraction; in the higher vibrations of its envelope as Repulsion, and within the kinetic skin wherein these forces play, the prakritic globes, planets, were born.

Take our earth. Each atom is fourfold—whether of the static core or of the static gaseous envelope. Creation on it is limited to the kinetic skin, wherein the attraction of the lower and repulsion of the higher notes in each octave of vibration have full play. All things on it must have come from the chording vibrations of the atoms of the prakritic elementary substances and their envelope of ether. They may or may not have life or mind the ether atom may have lost its chord with its pranic envelope, or the pranic envelope may have lost its chord with the manasic; but the combination must have force or energy within it. It may have lost Mind and Life in acquiring it, or after acquiring it; but it had to have life before it could become prakriti.

All things in the prakritic world flow from the Life of the etheric and the Mind of the pranic worlds. Everything in the etheric world has life, and our unconscious personification or "vivification" of etheric life transferred into fauna or flora, or into force of any kind, has a natural explanation. The thrill of vibration in one octave through the differentiated consciousness of the universe by which the light was separated from the darkness, the lower from the higher, was all that was required to create each star and sun, and world, and all that in them is. And it was all good.

Each thing on every lower world was but the translation into form of the type of the next world (or plane) above. As each element on this prakritic type, so each combination of those elements into crystal or tree or animal is but the translation. The normal earth from the crystal to (the animal) man was pure, and clean, and holy. Sin had not entered.

How did it come?

On the vast manasic world there was "a special creation"—that of the Angel Man. The three planes of Spirit above were undifferentiated consciousness, but they were in different octaves of vibration, and these working on the three highest forms of differentiated consciousness (manasic matter) brought them to chording Vibration so that when they combined and reached their highest point in evolution they "created" the Angel (or manasic) man. He was the product in kinetic manasa of the three spiritual planes above him, precisely as the animal man was the product in kinetic prakriti of the three material planes above him. The latter was the "shadow" of the other.

The Angel-man had a material (manasic) body, but his energy life, and mind were spiritual. The animal man had a prakritic body, with energy, life and mind that were material.

So far all was good.

The animal man has four bodies—one of prakriti, one of ether, one of prana, and one of manasa. It may be true, and probably is, that his manasic body is not sounding in chord with his prakritic body, but only with those atoms of it which are in his brain and nerves; but that is immaterial—for future consideration.

The Angel man had but one body, of manasa, in which the spirit dwelt; but that body was identical in substance with the body that made the mind of the animal man. His manasic body joined the manasic body of the animal man, joined with it by entering into the animal man's mind, as easily as water from one glass is added to water in another glass, and the animal "man became a living soul," endowed with speech, while the Angel-man was given "a skin coat."

The prakritic body of the animal man was the result in prakriti of an etheric-pranic-manasic, or "astral" body, formed in accordance with the Universal Law. For what he was by nature, he could not be blamed. He stood naked and not ashamed before the Radiance. He did not make his astral body; he was the mere translation of it into prakriti, as all other created things were, and that invisible astral self (figuratively) stood at his right hand, moulding and shaping him.

But when the Angel-man entered his mind, all this was changed. He "knew Good from Evil." To his mind of manasa had been added the Spirit—the Atma-Buddhi's Consciousness of the three Spiritual planes. He has become "as one of us," said the Angel- men of the firmament, of Heaven.

He now held the seven planes and was a creator. Each thought and desire that, when an animal only, fell harmless, now created on the pranic and etheric world. Soon beside him, at his left hand (figuratively) there grew up a second etheric or astral body, that of his desires; and his prakritic body was no longer the product of the astral body on his right hand. It was the joint product of the left-hand Kamic astral body he had created, and the right hand normal astral body. He was no longer in harmony with the Radiance. He could no longer face it. He had created discord—Sin.

The pretty legend of the two "Angels," one on the right hand and one on the left, has its physical basis in this truth, but, of course, as a matter of actual fact, the normal and abnormal astral bodies are in mechanical union. It is the Kamic self-made astral body that remains from one incarnation to another, producing in joint action with a new normal astral body, a new physical body for the Inner-Self, or Angel taking the pilgrimage through the lower world.

All the Angel-men did not enter the animal men on the pranic etheric-prakritic globes; only a few. It was a pilgrimage through matter in which those who make it are meeting many adventures, but the legends are many, and have no place in the physics, although the legends are all founded on the facts of the physics.

Of the number of monads, willing to undertake the pilgrimage, only a few of those within the kinetic belt of the manasic globe have reached the pranic. Only a few of those within the pranic kinetic belts reached the etheric. And of all who have reached this earth, only a few may win their way back before the great day Be-With-Us.

The problem of man, and his relations to the universe, are an entirely different line of study from that of the Spiritual Monad, the over-soul of every prakritic atom. Each prakritic atom has what may be called a soul, its three-fold astral cause; and an over-soul, or the three-fold spiritual archetype, or causeless cause.

Every combination of these atoms, whether a knife, a leaf, an animal, an earth, a sun, or a star, has this soul and oversoul.

Once the idea of what is meant by these terms becomes clear, the difficulty in understanding them vanishes. The study of man is physical in its lower branches; metaphysical only in its highest and last analysis. The study of the Monad is metaphysical from start to finish. The two studies are apt to be confused, because metaphysically they are often joined for study, the teacher taking it for granted that the pupil fully understands the simple and easy physics of the problem of humanity.

This, in crude and bold outline, is the story of creation to the fall of man according to the ancient physics, translated into the words and phrases of modern physics. The latter, in the latest discoveries of modern science, seem to have stolen a shive from the ancient loaf in the expectation that it would not be detected. Each and every step forward that modern science has made in the past twenty years, each and every discovery of every kind in the physical field, has been but the affirmative of some ancient doctrine taught in the temples of the East before "Cain took unto himself a wife."

Chapter Ten

The Septenary World

In the physical universe we have the four informing physical globes, so that as a whole or in its parts, it is "a string of seven globes," reaching from the highest spirit to the lowest matter. The awakened Universal Consciousness in vibration —undifferentiated in the three globes above, differentiated in the four globes below—in its last analysis is all one. But there is a gulf between matter and spirit, radically dividing them, and in the physical universe we are concerned only with physics and physical laws, until we reach its outmost boundaries and come in touch with the spiritual planes beyond.

This is the view of the universe at first glance, as in the smaller universe of this earth we at first see only its solid and liquid globes. And even after the discovery of the gas, we do not apprehend its important work in and behind the others until it has been pointed out to us. Nor do we at first apprehend the work of the spiritual in the material, and the object of metaphysics is to show, through the physics, the connection between them that the spirit works through matter; that where we can see but four there are seven beads on each material string; and that the last bead of each string is itself a chain of beads, the "chain of seven" applying only to the seventh manifestation, or prakriti, while the "strings" apply to the way in which they come.

On each unraveled string leading from our central sun down to a planet there are seven beads corresponding to the seven globes in the chain of each planet, each to each, yet not the same. There is a distinction, and it is no wonder there should have been confusion at first and a mixing of "strings" with "chains." The physics as they progress will clear this confusion away.

In the manasic globe, which is the first differentiation of that which forms the spiritual globes above, the resulting mind or manasa is mainly the differentiated Divine Mind of the highest. It has a "chain" of two globes only, itself and the Divine Mind globe, although its "string" of globes is four.

It is the perfected differentiation of the Buddhi in manasa that causes the formation of the pranic globes, which have chains of four and strings of five, and the full and perfect differentiation of the Atma in manasa-prana that causes the formation of the etheric globes, which have chains of six and strings of six. Consciousness, Buddhi and Atma are practically the same as the manasa, prana, and ether, each to each, only the latter are differentiated and the former are not.

Each of the three astral globes is the reflection in matter of the three spiritual globes beyond, each to each, and all to all.

The difference between matter and spirit is a difference in Motion only. Both are vibrating, so that both are in mechanical motion, from force without, like the waves of the ocean, but only the matter has what we may properly call motion of its own, or that produced from within—from the atom and each organism of it up to the ALL, as the vibration is from the ALL down to the atom. It is this centre of force in an atom, this motion outside of vibration, or rather beside it, which we call "differentiation." Brinton's "daring psychological speculation" that "mind was coextensive with motion" (from organization) was but a repetition of one of the most ancient axioms.

Take our solar etheric globe. It has two other globes of matter, consubstantial; a globe of prana and a globe of manasa. They are not beyond it, or beside it, but one with it, atom for atom. But what are they in reality? Globes of Atma, Buddhi, and Consciousness in which the atoms, having organized, are in motion, are they not?

Let this motion in this material universe cease, and matter would melt away and resolve into spirit. From spirit it came, to spirit it belongs, and to spirit it returns.

Behind each and every astral globe, whether the globe be but an astral atom, or an astral planet, or an astral world; beyond its physics there is a meta-physical globe, its cause, and that is the real globe, of which the astral is but a temporary phenomenon. Take a spiritual globe and differentiate it. The Motion resulting produces a material astral globe. Stop the motion; bring it to a state of rest. The astral shadow disappears. It was merely spiritual phenomena.

Each and every astral atom is a model in miniature of the material and spiritual universe. Each and every prakritic atom is the joint result of spirit and matter united and working together—of physics and metaphysics; and in its last analysis pure spirit; pure metaphysics.

Behind each and every prakritic atom of our earth there are six other atoms (or globes), three material shadows and three spiritual realities, so that it is a string of seven—the whole universe in miniature—material and spiritual. And all things combined and formed on a prakritic base are a chain of seven —whether a peach or a planet.

The "chain" belongs to the prakritic plane. The lines of descent from the Light through the star and sun to planet are "strings." The "chains" are beads of the same size strung on a thread. The strings are beads of different sizes strung on a thread. The beads of the chain are in coadunition—in the same space, as gas in water and the water in a sponge.

In metaphysics this earth can only be regarded as a chain of seven globes, its three astral globes in coadunition having their three spiritual doubles. Of course no one of the higher globes can be seen by the prakritic eye, but that is not to say the astral world cannot be seen by the astral eye in sleep, or by the person who qualifies himself for the astral world, through the development of his astral body. "No upper globes of any chain in the solar system can be seen," says H.P. Blavatsky in the Secret Doctrine (vol. I, p. 187), yet she means by astronomers, not by sages. And she does not mean the upper globes in the stellar system of Alcyone and its companions.

In pure physics the earth can only be regarded as a chain of four globes consubstantial and in coadunition—four in and three out. This makes seven, and the metaphysician when talking physics uses the metaphysical terms interchangeably and speaks of "the chain of seven globes" meaning in one sentence the four material globes making this earth; in another meaning the line of descent or string of beads of different sizes reaching down from the Divine Consciousness; and in still another the seven beads or globes of the same size in coadunition to form this earth chain. To the student who is thoroughly grounded in the eastern physics this interweaving of the physical and metaphysical presents no difficulties; but to the western mind just beginning the study it is a tangle.

We can now see what is meant by illusion, or Maya, and understand why such stress is laid upon it by every teacher.

Take the physical side first. The motion of a top gives it bands of color to our eyes that it does not have at rest. They are temporary and not permanent, a result of motion merely; illusion and not reality.

The motion of the material atoms of the four planes, in harmony with their vibration, a motion the spiritual world does not have, produces all material phenomena. This is of course within the kinetic belts, for above or below them there is no change, and its phenomena are the mere change in relation of one atom to another caused by motion. The changes are not real. They disappear when the motion stops. They have no existence in matter above or below the belt.

All phenomena of every kind are as much an illusion as the supposed bands of colour around the top. The illusion is the result of changes of relation in differentiated atoms caused by their motion. Without this motion the four material globes would dissolve into the atomic dust of the manasic world, with all that is within them. The whole material universe is all illusion; a mere temporary relation of its atoms through motion, without Reality or permanence.

What then is real? What is not illusion? That which is beyond the physical, that which is its cause and root; broadly, the metaphysical, which is not the result of differentiated atoms through relation. What was real in the top is real here. What was illusion in the top is illusion here.

The meta-physical or spiritual (the terms are interchangeable) does not have to pass beyond the manasic globe to get on the solid ground of reality. The spiritual world is here in every physical atom and in every aggregation of them; in every planet, sun, and star; for they are seven, each and every one, not four. Behind the illusion of one atom or many, whether here or on Alcyone, there is reality and permanency in the undifferentiated cause, the spiritual archetype, the three higher beads on the string which are the proper study of metaphysics.

Chapter Eleven

Stumbling Blocks in Eastern Physics

The Western student of the ancient Eastern physics soon meets serious stumbling-blocks; and one at the very threshold has in the last half century turned many back. In beginning his study of the solar system, the pupil is told:

The first three planets—Mercury, Venus, and the moon—are dead and disintegrating. Evolution on them has ceased. The proof of this is found in the fact, that they have no axial rotation, Mercury and Venus always presenting the same surface to their father, the sun, and the moon the same surface to its daughter, the earth.

This is a concrete statement of physical fact at which the Western student protests. If in the whole range of Western astronomical science there is any one fact that he has accepted as absolutely proved, it is that Mercury revolves once in 24h., 5m., 30.5s., and Venus once in 23h., 21m., 22s. He would as soon credit a statement that the earth has no axial rotation as that Mercury or Venus has none; and if he continues his study of Eastern physics it is with no confidence in its accuracy, and as a matter of curiosity.

The statement that Mercury, Venus, and the moon "are dead and disintegrating," the former two "always presenting the same surface" to the sun, is the basis for an elaborate superstructure, both in the physics and the metaphysics of the East. It is used in physics to explain how the "evolutionary wave" came to an end at the perfection of the mineral on Mercury with the loss of its axial rotation; how the "wave" then passed on to Venus with the seed of the vegetable kingdom, where the vegetable evolution ended with the loss of axial rotation; how from Venus it leaped to the moon, mother of animals and controller of animal life, with the seed of animal life in the vegetable; and how finally it came to the earth, when the moon ceased to revolve, bringing in the animal the seed of man. Here man will be evolved and perfected. Man has not yet been "born" on this earth, they say. He is still in a prenatal or embryonic condition within the animal.

The lunar Pitris, the men-seed, have a physical reason for being, if this evolutionary theory be true; none if it is not. Axial rotation is necessary in evolution, the ancient physics teaches, which must cease with it. The reasons for this are too lengthy to give here. Briefly, the rotation makes the electrical flow and a thermopilic dynamo of each planet.

The ancient astronomical teaching is absolutely true. There will not be a work on astronomy published in Europe or the United States this year, or hereafter, that will not state that "Mercury and Venus revolve on their axes in the same time that they revolve around the sun," which is another way of saying that "they have no axial rotation, always presenting the same face to the sun," and an inaccurate way of presenting the truth. The screw that holds the tire at the outer end of the spoke does not revolve "once on its axis" each time the wheel revolves. Run a cane through an orange and swing it around; the orange has not revolved "once on its axis." Nor does the stone in a sling revolve "once on its axis" for each revolution around the hand. The motion of Mercury is identically that of the impaled orange or the stone in the sling. It has no axis and no axial rotation. The modern astronomers, detected in pretenses to knowledge they never possessed, let themselves down easy.

This "discovery," of no axial rotation by the interior planets, made by Schiaparelli and confirmed by Flammarion in 1894, has since been fully verified by our Western astronomers. All the new astronomies accept it. But the admission of astronomical "error," to speak politely, comes too late for the student it turned back from his study of Eastern physics. He cannot regain his lost faith and lost ground.

Thirty years ago Proctor made it clear to Western students that the orbit of the moon was a cycloidal curve (a drawn-out spring) around the sun, the earth's orbit being coincident with its axis; and that the moon was, astronomically and correctly, a satellite of the sun, not a satellite of the earth. This has been the Eastern view and teaching from time immemorial.

The Eastern distinction between father Sun and mother Moon, and the classification of the latter as a planet, did not disturb the Western student. He understood that. It was the "absolute accuracy" of modern astronomers in regard to the length of the day on Mercury or Venus, which the astronomers declared had been corrected down to the fraction of a second, that made it impossible for him to accept the Eastern physics when the latter squarely contradicted his own.

This was but the first of many similar stumbling-blocks in the path of the student of Eastern physics.

> "Few were the followers, straggling far,
> That reached the lake of Vennachar;"

and when they did, this was what they had to face:

"The planets absorb and use nearly all the solar energy—all except the very small amount the minor specks of cosmic dust may receive. There is not the least particle of the sun's light, or heat, or any one of the seven conditions of the solar energy, wasted. Except for the planets, it is not manifested; it is not. There is no light, no heat, no form of solar energy, except on the planets as it is transferred from the laya center of each in the sun to them. The etheric globe is cold and dark, except along the lines to them—the "Paths of Fohat" [solar energy]. Six laya centers are manifested in the sun; one is laid aside, though the wheels [planets] around the One Eye be seven. [This alludes to the moon, whose laya center in the sun is now also that of the earth; but it is considered as a planet]. What each receives, that it also gives back. There is nothing lost."

"That settles it," says one student; and the others agree. Of the hundred who started,

"The foremost horseman rode alone,"

before the next step was won.

In the light of the tardy but perfect justification of the first stumbling-block, this statement may be worth following out, "to see what it means," and how "absurd" it can be. An etheric globe; cold as absolute zero, dark as Erebus, with here and there small pencils of light and heat from the sun to the planets —just rays, and nothing more—is a very different one from the fiery furnace at absolute zero of the modern physicist.

On a line drawn from the center of the earth to the center of the moon there is a point where the "weights" of the two bodies are said in our physics exactly to balance, and it lies, says our physics, "2,900 miles from the center of the earth, and 1,100 miles from the surface." This is the earth's "laya center" of the Eastern physics. It is of great importance in problems of life; but it may be passed over for the present.

Between the earth and the sun—precisely speaking, between this laya center and the sun—there is a "point of balance," which falls within the photosphere of the sun. This point in the sun is the earth's solar laya, the occult or hidden earth of the metaphysics.

A diagram will make this clearer. Draw a line from the laya center in the sun to that in the earth. Draw a narrow ellipse, with this line as its major axis, and shade it. At each end of the axis strike the beginning of an ellipse that will be tangent. If positive energy is along the shaded ellipse, negative energy is in each field beyond—earth and sun. This is a very crude illustration of a fundamental statement elaborated to the most minute detail in explanation of all astronomical phenomena; but for the moment it will do.

The point is that along this axial line connecting the laya centers play all the seven solar forces—light, heat, electricity, etc.—that affect the earth, and on every side of this line is the "electric field" of these forces. To this line any escaping solar energy is drawn, as the electricity of the air is drawn to a live wire or magnet. But there is little or none to escape. From the laya point in the sun to the laya point in the earth, the solar energy is transferred as sound is carried along a beam of light (photophone), or electricity from one point to another without a wire.

To the advanced student of electricity the ancient teaching is easily apprehended; to others it is difficult to make clear. These laya centers, it says, are "the transforming points of energy." From the earth laya to the solar laya centre, the energy, we may say, is positive; beyond both the solar and the earth laya centre, in the fields touching at them, it is negative — or vice versa. The line connecting the layas is the "Path of Fohat"—the personification of solar energy.

This is a very crude and brief way of putting many pages of teaching, but the important point is that this line between the layas is one of solar energy, with a dynamic "field" of solar energy, elliptical in shape, connecting with the reverse fields at the laya points. These "dead points" are the limits of each electric field, which "create", we say in electrical work, opposing fields beyond them.

Each one of these planets has its laya centre inside the sun's photosphere. Each planet has a line of solar energy with its "field" of solar energy—not only a wireless telegraph, but a wireless lighting, heating, and life-giving system. These six solar laya points are the six "hidden planets," the earth and moon being one, of the ancient metaphysics. The moon is the one "laid aside." In their reception of energy from the sun, it is as if the planet were at the solar laya point, or connected with it by a special pipe-line. The position of these six planetary laya points in the sun is indicated by the position of the planets in the heavens, and they may often influence or modify one another. If Mars, Jupiter, or Saturn is anywhere near conjunction with the earth, not only will a part of their "fields" be joined, but their laya points in the sun will be modified.

The physical basis of the old astrology was the physical interferences of these fields of solar energy; and what it depended on mainly in its work was the position of the six hidden planets, or laya centers, which was shown by the position of the planet with reference to the earth. That the planets themselves affected any one or anything on this earth, no real astrologer ever believed; that their position in the heavens indicated certain changes and modifications of the flow of solar energy to the earth, they knew from their knowledge of physics. "The twelve houses are in the sun," says Hermes, "six in the north and six in the south." Connect them with the zodiac, and the position of the planets shows the interferences of the solar currents.

The one objection to this ancient theory is that it does not present enough difficulties. The present value to science of the many theories in relation to the sun is the impossibility of reconciling any two of them, and the fact that no two theorists can unite to pummel a third. This ancient theory does not call for any great amount of heat, light, or energy in any condition to keep the Cosmos in order—not even enough for two persons to quarrel over. It merely turns the sun into a large dynamo connected with smaller dynamos, and these with one another with return currents by which "there is nothing lost." In its details, it accounts for all facts—neatly, simply, and without exclamation points. It is so simple and homespun, so lacking in the gaudiness that makes (for example) our light and heat less than the billionth part wasted on space always at absolute zero, that we may have to wait many centuries to have it "verified" and "confirmed" by our Western Science. That it will be "verified" in time, even as the first stumbling-block has been removed at the end of the nineteenth century, its students may at least hope.

> The lesson, if there is one, is that the Western student of Eastern physics does not ride an auto along asphalted roads. Hemustownhimselfandnotbeownedbyanotherman,oreven by "Modern Science."